How to SELL Life Insurance in 45 minutes

The EMERALD Way

By

Mitash Bhattacharyya

MBA, ALP-IIMA

Disclaimer: This book does not claim that everybody can sell Life Insurance in 45 minutes – it only says, to demonstrate a proper sales process to sell life insurance minimum 45 minutes is required.

Edited By

Anumita Bhattacharjee
MBA – SILVER MEDAL WINNER

PREFACE

The idea hovered around the pain of the Insurance Agents to sell a Life Insurance Policy to a Client. Because the Companies and their Development Officers / Unit / Sales Managers do not give the Insurance Agents enough time to understand the Business and not enough of Sales Training to build the selling skills, so there is a need for a handbook with defined process and tips for the insurance agents to refer to in whatever stage of sales process he is in.

"The Golden Compass: The reasonable man adapts himself to the world. The unreasonable one persists in trying to adapt the world to himself. Therefore, all progress depends on the unreasonable man". George Bernard Shaw.

As an Insurance Agent, you always wanted FREEDOM of Financial Independence. As a Sales / Unit Manager you wanted your agents to be successful from day one.

But what if you had access to a book that described how others in your position have used proven techniques to sell Life Insurance and climb up the ladder in MDRT Circle – how about a BOOK which guides you step by step to climb the ladder of success.

Any Insurance Agent will say: "I want that book!" However, we could not find it. We could not find the RIGHT TOOLS to sell Life Insurance. Fortunately, what we did find were stories from our colleagues across the world - success stories, brilliant personal achievements in shortest possible time and we wander how they can do it – what is the MAGIC.

After observing, training a lot of insurance agents in various parts of the world – the proven FORMULA is now within your reach.

This is to help each Life Insurance Agent to build their insurance career within the shortest possible time. I wish all of you Best of Luck

Mitash Bhattacharyya

MBA, ALP-IIMA

CONTENTS   PAGE

This Book is dedicated to

Mr. K.K. Sheri

Who dedicated his life

to train

Life Insurance Professionals

« Chapter 1 »

How to Earn more ………

"The habit of saving is itself an education; it fosters every virtue, teaches self-denial, cultivates the sense of order, trains to forethought, and so broadens the mind."
— T.T. Munger

A simple fact that is hard to learn is that the time to save money is when you have some – Joe Moore

"If you're saving, you're succeeding."
— Steve Burkholder

You have picked up this book for a reason. And the reason is to Earn more Money and be Successful at every Step you take. Yes, you are just in time to decide for yourself to change your life with this uncommon book. Why uncommon – you will discover it when you keep reading it – it excites you – because it's all the current situation you are passing through. I know it's a High-Pressure Zone that you are passing through.

If you are a Life Insurance Agent / Advisor – this book will help you step by step to understand the tips of selling a Life Insurance Policy maintaining full Compliance.

If you are a Sales Manager / Development Officer / Unit Manager of a Life Insurance company – this book is going to help you to understand the way you need to guide your team to build up their Skills & Competencies.

Now let's start with our purpose of how effectively and effortlessly we can sell a Life Insurance Policy in 15 minutes.

First, Congratulation! You have chosen the right business option – to become an Insurance Advisor. Very few careers are there in the world – where you're earning is directly proportional to your effort. Most of the time, you will find that the Insurance Advisors fail to achieve what they dream. The reason is they are putting their best EFFORT but not the <u>CORRECT EFFORT</u>.

LUCK is all about

L = Labour

U= Under

C = Correct

K = Knowledge

Correct Effort translates into RESULTS – Your Dream Earning.

In this book, we will be talking about the Correct Effort, the International Best Practices and the Key Steps which will help you to climb successfully up towards MDRT Circle.

When you have chosen this Career – many people might have discouraged you – that's good – for the time being they will not concentrate on you and your efforts. So, prepare yourself now with all the skills required to prove to the entire World – that Success means YOU.

You create a benchmark in your family and in your friend's circle and prove that your decisions are always RIGHT. I am here, by your side to guide you step by step to prove this. Never let yourself down. Under any adverse circumstances – You must win. You must create a benchmark that you are the WINNER.

"It's great to play a game where the RESULT is UNCERTAIN – but I have to WIN that remains CERTAIN" – Mitash

"Play to Win and Win to play" should be your mantra while you are in the field. Keep one thing in mind, you are working for yourself. You are your BEST Competitor. So every day create a new benchmark for your self – it will help you to propel further inch by inch and that determines a WINNER.

In this book – we will discuss step by step how to find the right customer, methods to identify their needs, how to present a plan, how to handle their objections & clarify them to their satisfaction and then close a deal. So, carefully take note of each crucial point, understand it to the core and change your action accordingly. So, let's start with the Concept of Business ......

Understanding Sales Process

Market Segmentation

Prospecting

Pre-approach

Approach

Need Analysis

Sales Presentation

Objection Handling

Negotiation skills

Close A Deal

Policy Delivery

Service after Sales

Let us know in sequence

Selling Process of a Seller

As an Insurance Agent, you need to follow the SALES PROCESS Step by Step

Now the Client (Buyer) also is having a BUYING Process

Buying Process of a Buyer

This is how a BUYER decide to buy something

Now understand Your Best-Selling Process should be equal to the Best Buying Process of the Buyer

Best Selling Process = Best Buying Process

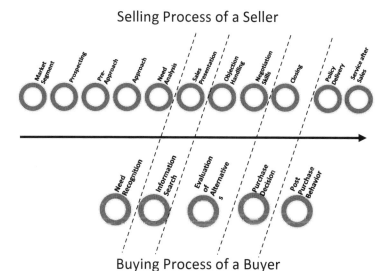

So as a Seller you always need to MATCH the Buyer's Buying Process – the dotted lines are various stages of the ***Selling – Buying Process*** – do not jump until and unless on stage is complete – Buyer's take some time to go to the next stage – accept that

« Chapter 2 »

The Concept of Business & Market Segmentation

Never be afraid to sit awhile and think. ~Lorraine Hansberry,

No matter where you go or what you do, you live your entire life within the confines of your head. ~ Terry Josephson

You and I are not what we eat; we are what we think. ~Walter Anderson, *The Confidence Course*, 1997

Read the above three quotes carefully and absorb them – before you proceed with this chapter. It is very true – that where we need to think more - rationally there we don't give time to ourselves and where we need to take quick action – we keep on spending a lot of time thinking irrationally. The Result is predictable…. status is unsuccessful…..we don't know the PROCESS " How To …" make the RESULT. Predictable.

The interpretation of the word LUCK now comes into this picture. Most people think that successful people are lucky – LUCK has favoured them.

Wrong. LUCK is ….

L = Labour

U = Under

C = Correct

K = Knowledge

So, people who are successful – they have really put a hard labour under correct knowledge at the appropriate time to become successful. They THINK RIGHT and then ACT RIGHT at the RIGHT TIME – that makes all the difference in their life.

So, in this chapter – I will make you THINK about your business.

What do you mean by the term BUSINESS? or let me put it this way ...

You need ONE thing to do BUSINESS ... if you do not have that ONE thing you cannot do business – you will be OUT of Business. What is that?

Think, think – got it?

MONEY (Capital)

SKILL

WILLINGNESS

PRODUCT

MANPOWER

SOFT SKILL

GOOD MANAGEMENT

All the above answers are WRONG.

To be in BUSINESS you need only ONE thing – without that, you are out of business and that is CUSTOMERS. Yes, dear CUSTOMERS.

BUSINESS = CUSTOMERS

(Business is equal to Customers - Never forget this)

The more business you want – the more customer you need

Think of a situation – I have given you plenty of Capital, Trained Manpower, Superior Products Excellent Management Team, solid IT Support and I have taken ONE COMPONENT OUT from you that is your CUSTOMERS (who are willing to stay with you). Can you be in BUSINESS? To-day CUSTOMERS are the crucial determinant factor – who decides who will be in business.

7

So how many CUSTOMERS do you have?

Yes, I am only asking about the NUMBER – no other description.

Let me be very precise about the definition of CUSTOMER in a Life Insurance Business.

If you have got a check from a customer as the First Year Premium – it is NOT-A-SALE. It is a breakthrough – **the FYP is just a sales breakthrough** – the sale will be completed when the LAST PREMIUM CHECK will be paid maybe after 10 / 20 or 30 years from now as per their choice of term.

Now tell me how many such CUSTOMERS you have who are ready to pay their last check …. or just to make a sale you told them to pay only for next three years or even maybe for just one year.

Now tell me how many such CUSTOMERS you have who are ready to pay their last check – this number determines YOUR QUALITY of SALE.

In to-day's business QUALITY is a pre-requisite to enter into the market, it's Your QUALITY of TRANSACTION – it's the minimum requirement to stay in the business or in other words – the customer will allow you to be in business as long as you serve him some QUALITY and the day he finds a BETTER QUALITY anywhere else – he will leave you. So, it is very important to give QUALITY SERVICE to the customer at the right time rather misselling (selling by telling wrong things)

Misselling will kill your business.

I know there is huge pressure from the top to perform – but if you do not remain in business – the company also do not remain in business in the future.

So, to be in business you need CUSTOMERS – and LOYAL CUSTOMER – who will stay with you for the next 10 / 20 / 30 years and above. Now keep one thing in mind – this business grows over a time – carefully you need to nurture this business.

At times you may feel frustrated – because you may not make a deal – that does not mean everyone has stopped buying Life Insurance Policy. It is you who could not find the RIGHT CUSTOMER.

So, in this business PLANNING is very Important and people give very little time for planning this business. Once they complete the mandatory Pre-Licensing Training – they undergo Product training from the company and then they jump into the business without much thought. Rather the Sales Manager asks for immediate business from your natural market (Friends & Relatives) – and you have no time to think and start at random to pick up a check as quickly as possible.

This pressure will be there – but you must be smart enough to move in the right direction to find the right customer.

Let's understand – how to find the RIGHT CUSTOMER – how do they look like, what are their habits – so that we can easily identify them in the crowd.

Now examine the pyramid (All figures are Annual Income)

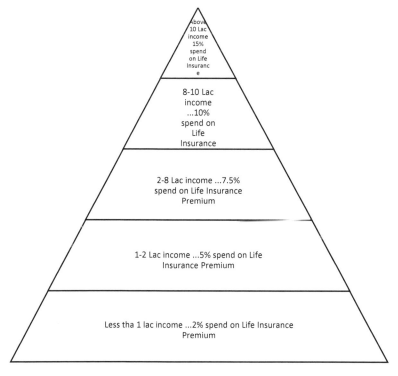

Mitash Bhattacharyya

2% , 5 % , 7.5%..... are indicative percentage of spending towards life insurance premium based on their annual income

.(Rs 1 Lac = US$1515

Rs 8-10 Lac = US$ 12122 – 15152

Rs 20-50 Lac = US$ 30304 – 75756

Rs 1 Crore & above = US$ 151515 & above …. annually

US$ 1 Million = Rs 66,055,000/- approx. when this book was written)

(If You are not from India – just look at the Maths – Not the Currency …in Your country the math remains the same)

You will find – people with Family income (NET take home after standard deductions) less than Rs 1 Lac – normally spend 2% of their income as Life Insurance premium i.e. a person whose net take home annually is Rs 1 Lac will pay around Rs 2,000 as the annual premium. If you show him a rosy picture he will still stretch to Rs 10,000 – but over a period, the policy will lapse.

WHY? Think this way – what is the average household expenditure in a month for a husband, wife and a child going to school. Roughly around Rs 8,000 is yearly Rs 96,000. Out of Rs 1 Lac - Rs 96,000 is yearly expenses. Now think of any Medical emergency, Festivals, Wedding invitation, birthdays – they are just left with Rs 4,000. Now if you are at this position can you pay the premium or will you try to save this emergency cash Rs 4,000 with you for emergency and other expenses. Have you noticed – they don't have any savings.

Now in the pyramid – if you go up – you will find that people – whose Family income (Income of all the people in the family put together – net take home / net profit from business) is Rs 1.5 -2 lac – they normally spend around 5% i.e. Rs 7,500 to Rs 10,000 as their annual premium. So, it is advisable to start your business from an income bracket of Rs 1.5 Lac and above. Why – because the household expenses will be around Rs 8,000 to Rs 10,000 i.e. Rs 120,000 annually. So, they will be having a disposable income of around Rs 30,000 – wherefrom they can give Rs 7,500 to Rs 10,000 as premium and rest can be their saving for an emergency and for their festival, holidays and gifts.

I will personally suggest – if you have a database of a customer whose family income is more than Rs 2 lac annually – your long-term income is absolutely secured.

Now the problem is – how to understand which family has a Rs 2 lac above income???

Let me give you two different cases.

Case One: A family with a husband and wife and a child 5-year-old living in their own house. Both the parents are working. They have a small hatchback car + a motorcycle/scooter. They indulge themselves in expensive dress materials, go to dine in good restaurants, go on holidays once a year. What do you think of their annual Family income????

Case Two: A Family with husband and wife and a child 5-year-old living in a rented house. The husband is working in a factory – has a cycle, normally buy one set of dress in a year for their child, do not have the scope to go a restaurant, cannot think of a holiday. Can you guess what is their annual Family Income????

Or – whom should you approach for a policy? You are correct the First family. But why – what have you observed that makes you decide to call the first family?

Yes, you have observed their **LIFESTYLE – their habits.** This is a clear determining factor.

LIFESTYLE is a LEAD INDICATOR

Let's have another case

Case Three: A family husband and wife and a 5-year-old child along with their parents (i.e. Husband's father & mother) living in their own house. The old man is suffering from cancer. The old lady is suffering from arthritis. The gentleman work in a government organisation and his wife is a homemaker. The gentleman travels on a bus to go to his office. They have not gone for holidays in the last 3 years. They always try to avoid a social function

Now – do you think – he is able to give premium? What's your gut feeling? A bold "NO" right – because the gentleman is in a tight condition. Even if you talk to him about critical illness & hospitalisation benefits coverage – he is not able to decide anything.

If I tell you to choose between Case two & Case three – whom do you approach.

If your answer is Case Two – you are wrong

If your answer is – I will not approach both the cases – then you are RIGHT.

You might feel bad – what to do with Case two and Case Three – they don't have money – but still we can help them – no, not by selling a policy – but you go back and join the Corporate Social Responsibility group of the Life Insurance Company you represent. The CSR group always come forward to help people who are in distress – join the group and do some Nobel work.

Among all the three cases – only Case One is a **TARGET SEGMENT**.

So, to identify a Target segment you need to observe few things

1. **LIFESTYLE of the Customer**
2. **LIABILITIES of the Customer**
3. **NUMBER of EARNING MEMBERS in the Family**

If both the member of the family is working and the Lifestyle is High (Show-off) and liabilities (liable expenses like Loans, Medical expenses, EMI, Credit card revolving credit etc.) are low – then this family is having a **GOOD DISPOSABLE INCOME. This family is the right segment.**

On the contrary, both the members of the family are working with high Lifestyle and high Liabilities – not at all a good segment to concentrate. If a family showing off lifestyle with a huge credit risk in the market – it's a risky customer for you.

The game of Life Insurance - is to find a customer with High Income (both working or high net worth businessman) and Low Liability. The high performing Agents / Advisors are BEST - at finding out these types of customers – rest will be history. You are bound to become number one. So, you need to have a **List of at least 100 names with income more than Rs 2 Lac – preferably with two family members working – as a minimum parameter to start your Life Insurance Business – THIS IS YOUR RAW MATERIAL – <u>THE NAMES – The DATA.</u>**

« Chapter 3 »

Prospecting

You never know till you try to reach them how accessible men are, but you must approach each man by the right door. ~Henry Ward Beecher, *Proverbs from Plymouth Pulpit*, 1887

In the business world, everyone is paid in two coins: cash and experience. Take the experience first; the cash will come later. ~Harold Geneen

The superior man understands what is right; the inferior man understands what will sell. ~Confucius

The difference between Extra-Ordinary Person & Ordinary Person – is the Word – **EXTRA.**

An Extra-ordinary person is also an ordinary person – but he always attempts something EXTRA – that an ordinary person normally skips & avoid.

This Attitude of always doing something EXTRA transform an Ordinary person into an EXTRA-ORDINARY Person.

In this Chapter, we will discuss some activity in which a normal person in Life Insurance Business does not attempt.

Let's understand what PROSPECTING is

> **By definition:**

- "Prospecting is the **conscious**, directed and **continuing** activity of **finding, observing, identifying** and **qualifying people**."

- "Prospecting is the cornerstone of your sales business."

  Either you prospect, or you go out of Business.

So now you decide – what you should do to continue your Business – you must do PROSPECTING.

Normally you will find Life Insurance Agents typically go out of Business within first 90 Days – the reason they do not understand what to do Step by Step to Grow in this business and make it BIG.

As we have discussed earlier that

BUSINESS = CUSTOMERS

So, you need to find as many CUSTOMERS as possible.

MORE BUSINESS = MORE CUSTOMERS = MORE INCOME

What are the steps to find CUSTOMERS?

You cannot find customers just like that – there is a process to find them out – if you walk that extra mile to find them – they are there in **PLENTY, in Abundance.**

Problem is people do not put the RIGHT EFFORT to find them out.

As discussed in the last Chapter 2 – you need to find a **List of at least 100 names with income more than Rs 2 Lac – preferably with two family members working – now it's time to work towards it systematically.**

Step 1: Take a REGISTER – to write these names

Exercise:

List down 100 names with income more than Rs 2 Lac – preferably with two family members working.

Feeling bored to write down the names – it's a normal feeling – but still, you must do it before you proceed. I told you earlier remember

BUSINESS = CUSTOMERS

In Life Insurance Business NAMES are the RAW MATERIAL and NUMBER OF POLICIES are the finished product.

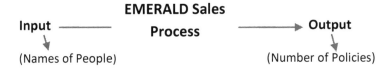

Input ————   **EMERALD Sales Process**   ————▸ **Output**

(Names of People)   (Number of Policies)

Let me clarify this:

To make a plastic pen – we require plastic granules as RAW MATERIAL and the final product is the PLASTIC PEN.

Can you make a PLASTIC PEN without that RAW MATERIAL – it's impossible!

That means there is an INPUT and there is an OUTPUT.

In the example of the PLASTIC PEN:

Plastic Granules are the Inputs & is processed through a Defined Manufacturing Process to get a Plastic Pen as an Output.

Input   Manufacturing Process   OUTPUT

(Plastic Granules)   (Plastic Pen)

Similarly, in Life Insurance Business: NAMES are the RAW MATERIAL (INPUTS) and they are processed through a Defined Sales Process (EMERALD sales Process) to get POLICY as an OUTPUT

INPUT   EMERALD Sales Process   OUTPUT
————————————————————————————————————▶
(NAMES)   (POLICES)

So more the Names = more Business for you

Because BUSINESS = CUSTOMERS

Now you are convinced, why you need that REGISTER to write those minimum 100 names of Prospects, with at least Rs 2 Lac and above income.

But All the 100 names are not CUSTOMERS.

Let's understand the Concept PROSPECTING more clearly

Your Current List of People (100 names) – all of them are not your CUSTOMER. Let me explain to you quickly – so that it becomes clearer to you.

SUSPECT ——————▶ PROSPECT ——————▶ CUSTOMER

(Doubt)   (Hope)   (Sure)

The 100 names you are writing – they are all SUSPECTS i.e. there is a DOUBT whether they will buy or not. They just qualify as per our parameter that we have decided "**income more than Rs 2 Lac – preferably with two family members working.**"

This does not mean All 100 people will buy. On the contrary – do you think ALL 100 of THEM will not buy? Right – some of them among these 100 names will show INTEREST (Hope) – they become your PROSPECT – out of these PROSPECTS – some will BUY & will make the payment. (No bounce Check – genuine payment) – they are your CUSTOMERS (Sure). So, the mathematics look like this:

SUSPECT ——————▶ PROSPECT ——————▶ CUSTOMER

(Doubt)   (Hope)   (Sure)

100   30   10

So, out of 100 Qualified names according to our parameter - "**income more than Rs 2 Lac – preferably with two family members working.**" – only 30 will show INTEREST and finally, **10 of them will <u>buy</u>.**

Now roughly calculate your earning with an average premium size of Rs 10,000:

10 x Rs 10,000 = Rs 100,000 Total Premium

Your Earning roughly 25% of Rs 100,000 = **<u>Rs 25,000.</u>**

To earn Rs 25,000 – what you have to do is:

<u>Step 1</u>: Take a REGISTER

<u>Step 2</u>: List down 100 names with income more than Rs 2 Lac – preferably with two family members working.

<u>Step 3</u>: Call them (All 100 People) – over Phone to take an APPOINTMENT and only 30 People has shown INTEREST.

<u>Step 4</u>: Meet ALL 30 People who are interested – and finally only 10 people bought the plan from you – and you Earn Rs 25,000.

Seriously tell me – is it difficult to meet 1 Person a DAY – so that in 30 Days you meet 30 People i.e. in One Month you will meet 30 People and 10 will Buy and you earn Rs 25,000.

I know you are laughing – because nobody in the trade sells 10 Polices in a month – and you are – RIGHT.

The reason they cannot sell 10 policies in a month is that they do not follow religiously all the above 4 Steps.

They don't carry a REGISTER of:

Qualified 100 names always

They don't meet 1 NEW Prospect A Day

They don't follow the EMERALD Method to SELL a policy in 45 minutes.

Yes, all that – we will discuss in the subsequent chapters.

Now in this process:

SUSPECT ⟶ PROSPECT ⟶ CUSTOMER

(Doubt)   (Hope)   (Sure)

100   30   10

Have you noticed something – that you need to MASTER now

Out of 100 People – 70 People said "NO" to you – that means YOU need to,.... Step 5

Step 5: **TRAIN your EARS** to HEAR the MAXIMUM NUMBER of "NOs" – if you want to be SUCCESSFUL.

The BIGGER the INCOME – the BIGGER the Number of "No's" you need to hear. The faster you complete the list of NOs from 100 names – you will have left out with "YES" List only – that's the BUSINESS. So now take the REGISTER:

Exercise:

List down 100 names with income more than Rs 2 Lac – preferably with two family members working.

I will help you out- to write this – Remember the Formula **F R I E N D S**.

F = Family, Friends

R = Relatives

I = Institutions (Your School, Your College etc.)

E= Employers (Biz-Men) & Employees

N= Neighbours

D= Doctors, Dealers, Dignitaries (Celebrities)

S=Strangers (People whom you don't know)

Prepare the list of 100 names according to this FRIENDS Formula

F= Get names among FAMILY members & your FRIENDS & their Parents

R= List down All the RELATIVES within our discussed parameters.

I= Institutions you know like your School (All Teachers) – go & meet them Your College Professors

E= Employers – people who are established Businessman or Top Management People & the entire Employee base – a huge potentiality.

N= Your Neighbours, Your Relatives Neighbours, Your Friends Neighbours.

D= Your known Doctors, Local Dealers, Celebrities, Eminent Professionals – Lawyers, CA, Film Maker, Actor, Singer etc.

S= This is the ACTUAL MARKET – where you will be spending the rest of your life if you want to succeed in this Business. To know these people, you need to continuously take **REFERAL** from the above categories. The STRATEGY – whenever you meet somebody over the Telephone or meet people personally – **ALWAYS ASK FOR AT LEAST 2 REFERRALS** - irrespective whether they are buying from you or not

REFERRALS is the Key to SUCCESS in this BUSINESS.

Since morning the moment, you open your eyes you see people around – keep taking REFERRALS – they may not buy a policy from you – but they will give you MORE LEADS to grow your business.

The POWER of REFERRALS

What is the advantage of REFERRALS vs COLD CALLS?

For e.g. Think of a situation:

One fine morning an Unknown person walks in & try to convince you about a Life Insurance Policy – would you like to make a payment – the answer is "no" – because you don't know the person – so you will try to buy some time from him by saying "let me think over " and the SALE gets delayed.

Now think – if that unknown person is a distant relative of your best friend – can you directly say "no" to delay the sales process – that's the power of a referral vs a cold call.

In a Referral case, people listen to you with more attention because you are related to a common someone. You get more privilege – MDRT Agents prefer this method than a cold call.

The REFERRAL technique can completely change the complexion of your business

Say for example:

Step 6: Out of All the 100 names – if you take only 2 REFERRALs in the 2nd Level you will get 200 Names (whom you don't know) – again from this 200 people (whether they are buying from you or not) – you take 2 REFERRALs – you will have 400 names.

So, taking REFERRALs is the KEY to Your SUCCESS. People who do not sell 10 policies in a month – they do not take 2 Referrals from each Customer – so their DATABASE does not GROW – so they don't see the SCOPE in this BUSINESS.

Now think when you have 400 DATABASE & 10 % will buy from you with an average premium of Rs 10,000 i.e.

40 x Rs 10,000 = Rs 100,000 – see how your income grows from Rs 25,000 to Rs 100,000 – the key, is to take 2 Referrals from each person irrespective of whether they are buying from you or not.

If you increase the number of referrals from 2 to just 3 referrals per person your DATABASE grows dramatically & so your income.

Now the **Tips of How to take Referrals** from a person. Remember 4 English WORDS that will help you to take Referrals quickly.

Step 7:

HELP

SUGGEST

ADVICE

OPINION

These 4 WORDS will help you get REFERRALS from people without bothering them.

Eg. Can you **please HELP** me to identify a Good Builder – the person who just bought a Flat or a piece of land – he will recommend his builders name to you – and the builder has MONEY to pay the premium.

Eg. Can you **please SUGGEST** a good Doctor for me – he will give you the name of his family Physician.

Eg. Can you **ADVICE** me who will be a good Civil Lawyer – ask somebody who is fighting a legal case.

Eg. What is your **OPINION** about the private tutor in your locality who teach Science to your child – take his number.

So, look for opportunity and ask relevant question using these words HELP, SUGGEST, ADVICE & OPINION – people are always ready to HELP, SUGGEST, ADVICE & put OPINION about others – you just need their contact phone numbers & ask the person permission to take his name as a referee – everybody willing is going to help you.

Step 8: Keep adding at least 10 NEW Names **Daily** – so in 365 Days – you will have a **DATABASE** of **3650 NEW Names in a year**

Now even 10% of this database of 3650 people buy from you i.e. 365 people will buy from you in a year @ Rs 10,000 as minimum premium which works out to

365 x Rs 10,000 = Rs 3,650,000 Total premium.

And roughly 25% is your Earning

25% of Rs 3,650,000 = Rs 912,500.

YOU ARE qualifying towards MDRT

Yes – small small steps & some <u>extra</u> planning & execution of the plan will make you an MDRT – an <u>Extra</u>-Ordinary Agent.

- You need to spend 70% to 80% your time prospecting. The success or failure you have in business will be in direct proportion to **your ability to prospect.**

There is a Formula for LIFE INSURANCE PROSPECTING – from the Underwriting Point of View. You know that you are the Primary Underwriter – so you have the responsibility to carefully select a CUSTOMER.

The Formula is **CHINA**:

C = Character (Good Character – no Moral Hazard)

H = Health (Good Health – no Physical Hazard)

I = Income (Regular Income – no Financial Hazard)

N = Need (Have reason to buy Life Insurance)

A = Accessibility (Can be in Regular touch)

So as an Agent we have 2 Responsibility

1. Sales Responsibility
2. Underwriting Responsibility

For sales Responsibility – we need to keep adding at least 10 names daily in the REGISTER.

For Underwriting Responsibility – we need to segregate the people using the formula **CHINA** – to get a **GOOD LIFE ONLY** for our company.

Adding 10 Names Daily will create a DATABASE of 3650 – and now you understand the potentiality of the earning.

<u>PROSPECTING HABIT 1</u>: GET NAMES OF PEOPLE FROM:

- **Personal Observation** – Observe your surrounding – who got a job, who got married, who got a child, who bought a house/flat etc. – they need an Insurance Cover.
- **Personal Acquaintances** – Your close people who are having liabilities in their shoulder.
- **Existing Policy Owners** – They are already sold to the concept of Life Insurance – but they need a cover at least 20 times (HLV = Human Life Value) of their Annual Income. Why? Say for example – if someone's annual income is Rs 2 Lac – he needs around Rs 40 Lac insurance (Term / Endowment combination). If he dies – his Family will get Rs 40 Lac & from Rs 40 Lac they can earn a Bank interest @ 7% of Rs 2.8 Lac. So, when the person was alive his annual Salary was Rs 2 Lac and after death his Family income will be Rs 2.8 Lac (which can cover inflation also – when he alive there may be 3 family members after his death only 2 family members ...but per person income is on the higher side.... that's the risk protection provision)
- **Centres of Influence** - A Centre of Influence is a fancy way of identifying people that have a hugely positive impact on your business. They often refer people and business to you and are actively recommending about what you provide and how you provide it. Every business needs a couple of these gems, and once you have them, you should bend over backwards to make sure they continue to think positively about you.
- **Referred Leads** – If you get a business or not – never fail to get at least 2 referrals as discussed before, remember HELP, ADVICE, SUGGEST & OPINION
- **Newspapers** - Look for Newspaper adv – which shop has announced a SALE or DISCOUNT – that means they will get New Customers – they will earn more – now they are on your list too.

Cold Canvas – Take help of the Marketing Canvas/Tent – go to a MALL or busy place – and keep taking names of people – do not discuss products. Sometimes people give away small inexpensive gifts to attract more people to the tent to get more names. Again, a caution – **do not discuss products**. Call them – take an appointment & then tell them.

PROSPECTING HABIT 2 – QUALIFYING THESE PEOPLE

Get as much information as you can to make sure they are real prospects for you.

- LIFESTYLE
- FAMILY SIZE
- TOTAL EARNING MEMBER
- FOOD HABITS
- WORK EXPERIENCE
- LIABILITIES
- FUTURE DREAMS
- SPECIAL EVENTS

PROSPECTING HABIT 3: Record This Information in the REGISTER

- Be Organized.
- The BOOK OF NAMES is an effective system to file the information of your prospects.

PROSPECTING HABIT 4: Get Introductions to People

- Try to meet people under the most favorable circumstances – preferably in their home & not in the office. (because Life Insurance is a product to protect people at home – so your sales presentation relates better at home – child's education, your retirement, daughter's marriage etc.)

- For every prospect or client served, whether the case is closed or not,

- ASK FOR REFERRALS!

PROSPECTING HABIT 5: China Egg...

- A prospect whom, in many cases, repeat calls simply develop into friendly chats that lead nowhere. ***Eliminate China Eggs***

- Do not waste time on people whom you keep calling on repeatedly but who never buy anything.

SUMMARY:

1. Take a REGISTER

2. Write 100 Names with income more than Rs 2 Lacs.

3. Call them (All 100 People) – over Phone to take an APPOINTMENT and only 30 People has shown INTEREST

4. Meet All 30 People who have shown interest

5. Always TRAIN your EARS to hear the MAXIMUM NUMBER of "NOs"

6. Take at least 2 referrals per person to increase your DATABASE.

7. Remember to use these words
    - **HELP,**
    - **SUGGEST,**
    - **ADVICE &**
    - **OPINION** - while asking for Referrals

8. Keep adding at least 10 NEW Names Daily – so in 365 Days – you will have a **DATABASE** of **3650 NEW Names in a year**

9. **PROSPECTING HABIT 1: GET NAMES OF PEOPLE**

10. **PROSPECTING HABIT 2: QUALIFYING THESE PEOPLE**

11. **PROSPECTING HABIT 3: Record This Information in the <u>REGISTER</u>**

12. **PROSPECTING HABIT 4: Get Introductions to People**

13. **PROSPECTING HABIT 5: China Egg...**

« Chapter 4 »

Pre-Approach

The telephone is a good way to talk to people without having to offer them a drink. ~Fran Lebowitz

You block your dream when you allow your fear to grow bigger than your faith. ~Mary Manin Morrissey

A friend is one of the nicest things you can have, and one of the best things you can be. ~Douglas Pagels

How to take an appointment in a professional manner.

"Sir, in your name there are two vacant slots available – one to-day evening from 7-8pm & the other tomorrow morning from 11-12am – which one is convenient for you so that we can send our Financial Planning Consultant – who can come down to your place & explain the plan in detail – which will take around 30-45 minutes "

The response from your Customer's end will either be positive or negative Once you have created a DATABASE – now it's time to ACT.

Always fix an appointment as per the favourite time of the Prospect to meet him.

Why an appointment –

- it's a Professional way to present yourself & your Business.
- It saves time

- It increases the chance of making a SALE

Every telecall that you make will not result in an appointment.

Initially, you will find the first 10 Tele-call you make – you do not end up with an appointment. That's normal – it is something like net practice in a cricket match.

I always recommend – take only 25 names from your DATABASE – who will never buy from you – call them first – so that your practice will be on, at the same time you know that they are never going to buy or give you an appointment. This will give you more energy to call the next 25 people – by that time you have almost done with the script.

Now look for a ratio for perfection – ideally, it should be 2: 1 i.e. if you call 2 people 1 should give you an appointment. Again, I am telling this ratio you cannot achieve initially. After 100 calls – just see how many Appointments you got that's your current ratio. Now work on that ratio to make it 2:1.

If you are little Tech savvy – it's recommended to send some direct mailer to your prospect to warm them up & then followed by the telecall for the appointment.

A note of caution – the direct mailer should be of professional quality – otherwise, it may backfire.

The purpose of your call is to get an appointment -- <u>not to sell</u> an insurance policy.

- In your tele-calling script - The words you use must be practiced and rehearsed until saying them becomes as natural as breathing.

- Knowing exactly what you are going to say will give you confidence and allow you to express yourself effectively.

<u>Good Telephone Techniques</u>

- Have a definite time for phone calls – call people between 11 to 1 pm & between 3 to 5 pm to take the appointment

- Address prospects by name with a salutation Sir, Mr. Mrs.

- Speak into the mouthpiece – speak slowly so that the person on the other side can understand all your words to form the opinion

- Be a good listener – when the prospect asks something – just be silent & listen carefully – normally they give you a clue to sell them – so **JUST LISTEN**

- Find a conducive place for making phone calls – avoid disturbances

A typical Good Script looks like this – which normally generate 2: 1 result i.e. out of 2 Calls you can get 1 appointment.

"Sir, I am ……. calling from ……………………… (Name of Your Company)

Is it a good time to talk to you"?

Wait for Customer response

If "NO" – ask – "What is the convenient time – so that I can get back to you "

If "YES" – proceed

Sir/Madam – you have been selected as one of our privilege customers to get a FREE DEMO of EMERALD way of building up wealth and protection for future

"Sir, recently we have launched a Wealth Building Program called EMERALD with some guiding principle – which helps you to achieve your Dream Bank Balance within a stipulated time frame to meet all your FINANCIAL needs & it provides you lump sum fund for your Comfortable retirement in future"

"EMERALD Planning Principles also helps you to reduce your tax burden to divert more funds towards creating wealth & protection."

If it is positive you have an appointment.

If it is negative – Prospects say "No I am not interested "

Just add one more sentence – "Sir, with your kind permission – can I give both your slots to the next standby Customer "– just be **silent** after this.

Watch for the REACTION

Normally people start getting a feeling of "losing out" something which is allocated to me.

The Prospect might immediately ask you "just tell me in a brief"

Your answer – "Sir, it's the expert who will be coming to your place" (it maybe you only)

Please note – just play the Role of a tele-caller – as if you really don't know what this EMERALD planning principle is all about. Only ask for which time slot he want to confirm for the meeting.

The **OBJECTIVE** of the tele-calling is only to get an **APPOINTMENT** – NOT TO SELL OVER PHONE.

Some do's and don'ts:

Do's

- Before calling anyone – rehearse the script at least 100 times – yes 100 times – till the script flows naturally for you. Think the actor you like the most – they put this effort to give their final shot.
- List down 25 names initially – whom you know they will not buy.
- Call them – this is your net-practice like a cricket match
- Once you are confident & got close to the ratio of 2:1 – start calling your DATABASE – your floodgates open up

Don'ts

- Do not call people between 8 to 11 am in the morning.
- Do not call from a place with a lot of noise from the background

« Chapter 5 »

Approach

Between saying and doing many a pair of shoes is worn out. ~Italian Proverb

A promise is a cloud; fulfilment is rain. ~Arabian Proverb

In skating over thin ice, our safety is in our speed. ~Ralph Waldo Emerson

Now it is ACTION TIME – physically you need to move and meet the Prospects. In the last Chapter – you made phone calls to make appointments – now you go meet them.

Between saying and doing many a pair of shoes is worn out. ~Italian Proverb

Keep the formula in mind:

- SPEED
- STAMINA
- COMMITMENT

These three letters will prove – what you TELL and what you DO are the same – that's what a PROFESSIONAL look like.

All the appointments you have will only transform into BUSINESS depends only on:

- How fast you meet all of them – SPEED

- How long you can maintain your SPEED – i.e. STAMINA
- And you are at everybody's doorstep – at the right time of the appointment – COMMITMENT

If you can prove these 3 factors to YOURSELF only – you are the next MDRT going to the USA.

DRESS and then ADDRESS

This is very important – first, you DRESS and then go to your Prospect to ADDRESS them about your Plans and Solution.

"The first four minutes of your initial contact are the crucial ones. It's the average time, demonstrated by careful observations, during which the prospect decides whether to continue or terminate the discussion." *Dr. Leonard Zunin*   *Psychiatrist*

Things That People First Notice About You

- **Appearance** – Clean save for gentleman & not too loud make-up for Ladies with hair well done

- **Facial Expressions** – the **SMILE** on your face is the most important factor which makes a clear difference. Just like some clothes fits you well – try to stand in front of the mirror to see which SMILE fits you best and then practice it in front of the mirror – until it becomes your second nature

- **Movement** – notice yourself in the mirror which GESTURES & POSTURES you look great – from now on you need to wear those gestures & postures. Take the help of your friend to identify – if you are demonstrating any bad gesture or posture that they don't like. Take this FEEDBACK – change yourself to your NEW LOOK & get accepted in the society.

- **Tone** – understand the TONE and tempo of voice. If you are using some very local tone – it will be difficult for you to make a breakthrough beyond that community. Always ask your friends to give you a feedback. They will give you an honest opinion.

- **Pitch of Voice** – Sometimes you will find people talking to you closely at a very high pitch – they could not understand themselves – but we internally feel annoyed. The same is the case with a Prospect. Practice a modulation of up and down and firmness in your pitch.

- **Words** – These are the most critical objects that complete a communication. Words carefully chosen can create a miracle. Scientifically our brain neurons only listen to words of other people & help us to react accordingly – so you understand – people will only respond according to your wish provided you have carefully chosen your words.

Appearing ON TIME for an appointment – is a WONDERFUL THING – it demonstrates PUNCTUALITY – you will never get a second chance to create the **FIRST IMPRESSION**

Your opening statement should be brief and to the point. You need to identify yourself and your company, state why you are calling and what action you want them to take.

People, in general, are not interested in Life Insurance. So, you can start something like this:

"Sir we are conducting a survey – would you mind discussing your Life Insurance needs". Normally the person will tell "I am not interested in Life Insurance".

"Thanks, Sir, you are absolutely right – our survey also reveals that 99% of people are not interested in Life Insurance – but everybody is interested to make money and build wealth".

You have three big goals when it comes to developing an opening statement that works. You want to:

1. Make it sound conversational.
2. Deliver it with confidence.
3. Get a favourable interruption--one that will put your prospect in control as soon as possible.

Do's and Don'ts to Gain a Favorable Impression

Do's

- Do be prompt for buying

- Do give a warm greeting with a firm handshake.

- Do avoid conversation relating to politics, race and religion

- Do stay enthusiastic. It's contagious. It attracts a favorable response.

- Do find something to praise.

- Do watch your posture and look your prospect in the eyes.

- Do make the prospect feel important.

Don'ts

- Don't mispronounce your prospect's name.

- Don't show impatience.

- Don't compliment unless it is believable

- Do avoid conversation relating to politics, race and religion.

Biggest Negative in Financial Adviser's Appearance

- Wrinkled Clothing create   85% negative impact

- Unsigned Shoes create   62% negative impact

- Poorly Tied Necktie create   58% negative impact

- Clashing Colors create   42% negative impact

- Poor Oral Hygiene create   50% negative impact

- Untidy Hair create   52% negative impact

Pointers for Dressing

- Your clothes must ...

- Look fresh and clean

- Fit your size and build

- Be comfortable

- Be-well coordinated

- Reflect your profession

Accessories to Avoid

- For Ladies: Avoid Cheap costume jewellery and imitation watches

- Sandals, slippers, too high heels and casual footwear.

- Belt buckles that have ornate designs (unless for casual wear)

- White socks for men (until & unless you are wearing a white trouser)

Now you know what to wear, how to wear and what to talk.

Exercise: Write down a script

1. Introducing yourself and your company
2. A hooking statement to create interest in the mind of the Customer
3. Rehearse, rehearse & rehearse

« Chapter 6 »

Need Analysis

Dreams are answers to questions we haven't yet figured out how to ask. ~X-Files

Every child comes with the message that God is not yet discouraged of man. ~Rabindranath Tagore

The safe way to double your money is to fold it over once and put it in your pocket. ~Frank Hubbard

SALES PRESENTATION – OLD CONCEPT

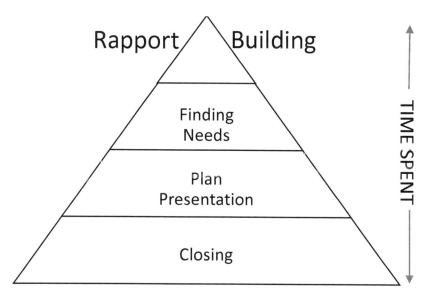

There are two school of thoughts – OLD CONCEPT & NEW CONCEPT in PERSONAL SELLING SKILLS.

The OLD SCHOOL OF THOUGHT believe that – give maximum pressure on Sales Closing – Less emphasis on building Rapport.

The NEW SCHOOL OF THOUGHT believes that put all the emphasis on building RAPPORT with the client – SALES CLOSING is just an outcome of the NEW RELATIONSHIP and this is true.

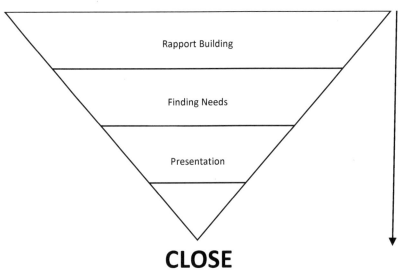

Very few people give stress on RAPPORT building – but it is the ultimate skill you need to build over a period – and it helps you in your professional as well as personal life. Think of a situation through Life Insurance Business – you know the renowned Police Officers, renowned Doctors, Film Actors, famous Playback Singers, Big Business Tycoons etc. And if you really build a rapport with them – at your personal level you get their help always apart from business when you are in problem.

The Cardinal Rule in Selling Life Insurance: Build A Relationship!

- Research indicates the buyer buys insurance principally because of a relationship with the financial adviser

- Establish yourself as a friend and a problem solver

- Emphasize the kind of service you offer as a financial adviser

Most People Want To:

- Improve something – like Lifestyle

- Maintain something – like their Car

- Reduce something – like their Worries and Life Insurance act here to reduce people's worry about Future

Rapport Building Technique

Probing Techniques: There are two kinds of questioning skill

- Start with **CLOSE ENDED Questions** – where the answer cannot be "YES' or "NO"

Something like "What have you planned for your Child's education?"

The client says: "DOCTOR or ENGINEER"

You ask: "You mean both?" (Humorously)

The client says "No actually we have not decided yet – he is too young – but definitely he will go for higher education"

- Follow with **OPEN ENDED Questions** – answer ends with "YES" or 'NO'

You ask: "so you will require A HUGE AMOUNT OF MONEY?

The client says: "YES"

- Come to an AGREEMENT –

You ask "So for the education you may require around Rs 15 lac ("Y" amount) after 14 years because your child is only 4 years now – so when he became 18 you require this money – and whether you present or absent at that time this amount is still required – RIGHT"

The client agrees: "YES"

You say : "If I show you a plan where you invest only "X" amount over a period of 14 years and it gives you a return of Rs 15 lac ("Y" amount) & that too irrespective of your presence or absence in your family and it guarantees Rahul's education (take the name of the clients son /daughter always – it creates better association with your Product and their Purpose.) – will you be interested to listen to the plan ? "

The client says; "YES" – so you got a commitment to listen to the plan.

Before I give the clue of how to use EMERALD Technique – let me clarify some basic conceptions about Marketing.

All marketers all over the world work on 3 basic words

1. **NEED**
2. **WANT**
3. **DEMAND**

Let's understand that clearly by taking an example:

Whenever we feel hungry we **NEED** - FOOD.

The design of the FOOD varies from place to place and from culture to culture.

So, if an Indian, an American & a Chinese are hungry – they also NEED – FOOD – but the design of the FOOD is different.

The Indian **WANT**: RICE or ROTI

The American **WANT**: BURGER

The Chinese **WANT**: NOODLES

Now comes the affordability (**DEMAND**) – if at a price point we find that we can sell maximum – normally Marketing Managers fixed that price.

Let's take an example:

If we do a survey among 100 Indian clients for the **DEMAND** for RICE or ROTI – and let's take we take 3 price point:

1.   RICE & ROTI THALI cost Rs 30
2.   RICE & ROTI THALI cost Rs 70
3.   RICE & ROTI THALI cost Rs 130

(THALI = PLATTER)

If we survey these 3-price points among 100 customers – the result might look like this

1.   If the price is Rs 30 –
     90 people out of 100 will buy – that means 30 x 90 = Rs 2700 revenue can be generated.
2.   If the price is Rs 70 –
     only 30 people out of 100 will but – that means 70 x 30 = Rs 2100 revenue will be generated.
3.   If the price is Rs130 –
     only 10 out of 100 will buy – that means 130 x 10 = Rs 1300 revenue will be generated.

So, if you are the businessman – what price will you keep – obviously Rs 30 per thali – because it generates maximum revenue.

So, if the price of RICE & ROTI THALI (Platter) is Rs 30 – there will be a **GOOD DEMAND.**

Summary of Marketing Concept: Whenever anybody is HUNGRY

■   - **Need**: They need **FOOD** – when they are HUNGRY

■   - **Want**: The design of the **FOOD** can be **RICE, ROTI, BURGER, NOODLES** – depending upon which segment we are catering to & what's their TASTE

■   - **Demand: At what price point the maximum SALES will be generated – is its <u>Affordability.</u>**

Remember this concept forever – we will require this concept during Sales Closing.

The CONCEPT OF EMERALD

EMERALD is an acronym to remember certain events – and you can seamlessly talk to the customer without thinking about what to say next.

E = Education of the Child

M = Marriage of the Child

E = Emergency

R = Retirement

A = Accumulation of Wealth

L = Loans & Liability coverage

D = Death of the Earner

Once you remember EMERALD - anybody you meet – you can immediately recognize their **NEED** and can immediately understand which PLAN they **WANT.**

When you probe a little for their commitment of investment – the price they are telling you beyond that its tight for them – you understand at this PREMIUM point your PLAN has a good **DEMAND** for this customer.

Now to understand the EMERALD Needs of various client write down their EMERALD needs at various stages of LIFE

- YOUNG PROFESSIONAL – what EMERALD need they have…….

- JUST MARRIED - what EMERALD need they have…….

- BIRTH OF FIRST CHILD - what EMERALD need they have………

- GROWN-UP CHILD - what EMERALD need they have………

- HIGHER EDUCATION OF THE CHILD - what EMERALD need they have….

- Children's MARRIAGE - what EMERALD need they have…….

- Their RETIRED LIFE - what EMERALD need they have………

- LAST DAYS OF LIFE - what EMERALD need they have…….

Every time you will find multiple EMERALD needs are there in various age bracket. See table

EMERALD FORM OF YOUR LIFE			
NAME:	AGE:	INCOME:	**SUM**
EVENTS OF LIFE	AFTER HOW MANY YEARS (POLICY TERM)	AMOUNT NEEDED FOR EACH EVENT	**ASSURED NEEDED FOR EACH EVENT**
1. EDUCATION			
2. MARRIAGE			
3. EMERGENCY			
4. RETIREMENT			
5. ACCUMULATION OF WEALTH			
6. LOANS & LIABILITIES			
7. DEATH			
TOTAL SUM ASSURED			

Please fill-up this format with every client – let them fill the amount they require for each event & after how many years they require that amount…. automatically after filling this format – people understand that they are Financially not well protected.

EMERALD events are the biggest events in life when lump sum amount of money is needed & some of these events come without warning…so be prepared.

Use this table as a thumb rule

EMERALD NEEDS	Status	When required	Total Amount Required	Type of Plan	Sum Assured	Premium Payment Term
Education						
Marriage						
Emergency						
Retirement						
Accumulation of Wealth						
Liabilities						
Death						

Take an example: A Couple with 3-year-old son, husband 30 years wife 28 years, both working, just bought an apartment for 6,000,000 – Home loan for next 30 years

EMERALD NEEDS	Status	When required	Total Amount Required (in any currency)	Type of Plan	Sum Assured (S.A.)	Payment Term
Education	Child 3 years	After 15 years when the child will become 18 for higher education	Say 2,000,000	Child's Education Policy	2,000,000	15 yrs.
Marriage	Child 3 Years	After 25 years when Child will be 28 years	Say 1,500,000	Marriage / Endowment Policy	1,500,000	25 yrs.
Emergency	Everything ok	Can't predict	Say 500,000	Rider Critical Illness & Hospitalization worth 500,000	500,000	30 yrs.
Retirement	Husband age 30	After 30 years when he will be 60 years of age	Say 5,000,000	Retirement Plan (For getting a monthly pension to sustain)	5,000,000	30 yrs.
Accumulation of Wealth	Husband age 30	After 30 years when he is 60 years	5,000,000	Endowment Plan Traditional or Unit Linked	5,000,000	30 yrs.
Liabilities	Home loan 6,000,000	Next 30 years is crucial	6,000,000	TERM Policy	6,000,000	30 yrs.
Death	Total liability: Monthly family Expense/ Education, Marriage & Home Loan		9,500.000	TERM Policy	9,5000,000	30 yrs.

Look at this person's life:

1. Has total liability: Education + Marriage + Home Loan = 9,500,000
2. So, he should immediately take a TERM Policy for 9,500,000 Sum Assured.
3. Why?
4. If he dies the next moment – the wife will get 9,5000,000 – and they will never be thrown out of their apartment, as wife can repay the loan at one shot plus she will be having extra money for the child's education & Marriage.
5. If the person still has more spare money based on his income – give him a retirement plan – post 60 years he can have monthly income to sustain.
6. After one or 2 years you can still approach the man to take an education & marriage policy
7. If he gets a promotion or increment – give him an endowment policy for accumulating his wealth.

Now based on the same concept work out the wife's policy or try to share their total liabilities among both using this chart

EMERALD NEEDS	Status	When Required	Total Amount Required	Type of Plan	Sum Assured	Premium Payment Term
Education						
Marriage						
Emergency						
Retirement						
Accumulation						
Liabilities						
Death						

By now you understand how to use this chart – so with your very next customer use this chart to show him his liabilities – take a blank copy of this chart – prepare it in an excel and take the print out.

How to calculate INFLATION and actual value required after a certain period.

Take the above example:

Education	Child 3 years	After 15 years when the child will become 18 for higher education	Say 2,000,000	Child's Education Policy	2,000,000	15 yrs.

In this example, then it is assumed that 2 million (Rs 20 Lac) is needed for Education after 15 years.

But the Value of Rs 20 Lac (2 million) will not be the same as today's value, INFLATION will eat up that value and actually it will be more COSTLY after 15 years.

So, first let's understand the concept of inflation in a very lay man's term.

Today with Rs 125 ($2 approx.) – if you can buy 5 pieces of mango, may be next year with the same amount of money you will buy 4 pieces of mango, and next to next year may be the with same amount of money you get only 3 mango....and after 15 years you may buy a picture of a mango with the same money.

That means to money loses its buying capacity for over a year.

Now take the above example. For the Childs's education the parents are thinking Rs 20 Lac (2 million) is ok for higher education as on date – but for the same education after 15 years the price of that same course will go up.

Now the question is ...so how we know how much it will be after 15 years.

Normally the inflation by thumb rule is around 10% each year, that means every year on an average the price of everything goes up by 10% and it is compounded annually.

So how to calculate the value in front of the Client.

Take a CALCULATOR, no your Smartphone Calculator will not do this job, so you need to carry a physical calculator or in your smartphone go to Google Play Store and download CITIZEN Calculator.

Now let's understand how to calculate the Future Value of an event.

Let's say with Rs 100 you get 4 mongoes this year – so if the inflation is 10%, then next year for 4 mango you have to pay Rs 110.

So, 10% increase means

Rs 100 will go up next year by Rs 110 more

Re 1 will go up next year by 110/100 = Re 1.1 right..simple unitary method (if you are still confused at this stage about the calculation, to ask someone at home or in office)

Step 1 : Now take the Calculator and just type 1.1 (on the display)

Step 2 : Next press " X" sign twice

Step 3 : Now press "=" sign 14 times (if the TERM is 15 years press one less than 15 i.e. 14 times "=" , if the term is 30 years then press "=" 29 times in the calculator) whatever is the factor coming just multiply it with the Present Value

See how much you get.....it is around 4.177 almost 4.18 approx. right

That means whatever you can buy with Re1 today will cost Rs 4.18 after 15 years...yes dear, it is around 4 times more.

So, for the education, the parents are thinking that Rs 20 Lac (2 million) is sufficient but it is for today not for after 15 years.

Now multiply the education price Rs 20 Lac X 4.18 = Rs 83.6 Lac

Yeah, life is tough PLAN IT WELL IN ADVANCE

Now if instead of 10% inflation is 15% then instead of 1.1 as a factor you have to consider 1.15 as the multiplier factor to understand

« Chapter 7 »

Sales Presentation

Try not to become a man of success, but rather try to become a man of value. ~Albert Einstein

Success consists of going from failure to failure without loss of enthusiasm. ~Winston Churchill

I couldn't wait for success... so I went ahead without it. ~Jonathan Winters

Sales Presentation is the moment when you must display your confidence and all your Solution i.e. the Plans are matching the **EMERALD** needs

The Concept of AIDA is another acronym to remember – what you should do now. These are 4 stages of Sales Presentation

A = Attention

I = Interest

D = Desire

A = Action

- **ATTENTION**

At this stage, which is the beginning of your conversation, say "Sir, if I could show how to solve all your financial liabilities and live a life with peace of mind, would you interested to look at the process."

These sentences are called Attention grabbing questions.

- **INTEREST**

In this stage, you must arouse customer's interest to listen to your solution.

"Sir, there is an easy Formula to cover up all your liabilities in life – would you like to see the formula."

After telling this, show him the EMERALD Form.

- **DESIRE**

DESIRE is the stage, where the Customer can correlate your solution with his needs.

After completion of EMERALD Form – the Customer will say "oh! I don't have that much money to cover up the whole EMERALD List" – you say, "I know, so I suggest you always go step by step – cover the liability which is coming up in recent future and gain at least 25% peace of mind – Sir don't attempt to cover everything in one policy".

"We have:

1. Child Policy for Education & Marriage (EM)
2. Some policy has Partial withdrawal (E)
3. Retirement Policy (R)
4. Whole Life / Endowment policy (A)
5. Term Policy (L, D)

Based on his immediate requirement – suggest to him "Sir, you start with this first"

Show this:

There are 2 ways to make money

1. **You Earn minus you spend and try to save**

   OR

2. **You Earn minus you save and spend the rest**

Which one do you think will help you to make money.

90% of people will earn the salary or profit, they will spend and then they try to save, and nothing is there in their hand to save.

And 10% of smart people will earn, set aside and invest in a life insurance policy and rest of the money they spend to fulfil their wish of having a peace of mind.

Life is a Project...gain control over it.

Saving is a discipline ...just like brushing your teeth in the morning. Save regularly, every month systematically to gain control over life.

- **ACTION**

This stage of the Sales Presentation – you must use 6 steps Objection handling process and minimum 5 trial closing techniques to CLOSE the Deal.

We will talk about that later in the next subsequent chapters.

Essentials of an Effective Presentation

- It must capture your prospect's instant and undivided attention. **(A)**

- It must arouse interest **(I)** by describing owner benefits and their advantages to the prospect.

- It must build desire **(D)** by winning your prospect's confidence.

- It must motivate your prospect to act **(A)** now

Remember

- People are not moved or motivated until they feel a certain INTERNAL TENSION.

- When a person can relate to a specific NEED for the CAUSE of a specific problem, that person begins to look for a SOLUTION.

- Keep the EMERALD form in front of the customer and ask relevant questions about what immediate event he needs to cover, like Child's Education first, then child's marriage and step by step help him to cover all the liabilities in His EMERALD List.

- Over a period normally a person will buy 3 to 4 policies to cover up His EMERALD List.

How to Present and Position your Plans to help Customer to decide and close the deal

Take up the first need (problem / purpose) and discuss the plan.

The biggest mistake Salespeople make is they put a lot of emphasis on the Plan but forget to emphasize the PURPOSE for which he should buy.

Discuss more about the problem / purpose – for example, if it is child's education – go deep ask the question, what kind of education they have in their mind, how much money will be required at the final stage of the Higher Education, how it cost now and how it will cost later. Let them feel their situation. If they don't provision for it now – the child may lose the opportunity because you are financially not prepared – will you allow your child to lose one academic year in his life , he will enter into his Professional life also one year later, the child will lose one year of his income...say " 100,000 " amount of yearly income...and if you start today with " 10000" amount you are gifting your child a secured future.

Always talk more about each purpose in the EMERALD List and magnify the problem going deep into it – not by talking more about your plan.

The more you can talk about their problem / purpose from the EMERALD List, the closer you will get to CLOSE the Deal.

Main three areas of a PRODUCT / SERVICES are

- FEATURES

- ADVANTAGES

- BENEFITS

- How it satisfies the BIG PICTURE in the CUSTOMERS MIND

Probe: "Would you like to know HOW - **Your family gets a Ring of Security** – & your liability do not touch them in case anything happens to you?"

- Advantage: "Choose cover level according to your liability"

- Benefit: "You are SECURED at every step"

- Feature: "Our product has a feature called FLEXIBLE LIFE COVER"

Probe: "Your Dream will never shatter – You always fulfil your desire – because your money retains its purchase power always - do you want to know - how?"

- Advantage: "It covers the Inflation every year"

- Benefit: "The purchase Power of Your Money remains intact"

- Feature: "Our Product has a feature called INDEXATION"

Probe: "No Tension about tax-deduction on maturity – interested to know – how is it possible?"

- Advantage: You put extra savings in the same fund, you put matured fund of other investment (FD, Mutual Fund etc.) in the same plan

- Benefit: All your future savings will have a tax-free maturity

- Feature: "Our product can help you to get a tax-free return on all your investments – through a feature called ADDITIONALITY".

Probe: "One account – Several withdrawals – like to know more in details?"

- Advantage: "Withdraw money whenever you require – works as an ATM (All Time Money)"

- Benefits: "Same policy works like a Bank Savings Account"

- Feature: "Our policy has a unique feature called PARTIAL WITHDRAWAL".

Probe: "Rotate a set of money for three years & let your FUND grow Faster than the average – want to see, how to do it?"

- How? – say, you want to invest Rs 15,000 as additional premium – so you buy the units at a price say, Rs 15 – you get roughly 1000 units

Now after 3 years you want to take out the same Rs 15,000 you have invested – let say at this time the unit is priced at Rs 30 each – so to take out Rs 15,000 you now need to sell only 500 units out of your 1000 allocated to you 3 years back & save another 500 units in your FUND. You can rotate Rs 15,000 for the first 3 years & take out on the 3rd year & keep on rotating & bag the extra units in your FUND – so your FUND grows faster than the average

- Advantage: Combination helps you to grow your FUND faster without investment

- Benefit: Make more money without further investment

Probe: "Any time hospitalization possible without any tension – no head-ache to family members – want more details"

- Advantage: Same policy covers your Hospitalization

- Benefit: You do not have to take a separate policy & pay additional policy charges

Feature: "Unique Hospital/Critical illness Benefit"

Probe: "Somebody is behind you to protect your family even in your bad financial phase – the cover continues as long as the fund permits – you want to know how you will get protected during your bad financial phase?"

- Advantage: Even if you are unable to pay – you are still covered

- Benefit: You are still covered in your bad financial phase

- Feature: "Our Paid-up feature is unique or do a partial withdrawal of your premium amount and continue till you recover from your bad financial phase"

Probe: "When you put other mature funds in the same policy as an addition – you save charges of other investment accounts – like to see how it works?"

- Advantage: You know them all – all charges are explicitly shown

- Benefit: You know how much money is going for investment

- Feature: "Our charges are explicit and transparent".

« Chapter 8 »

Objection Handling

An objection is not a rejection; it is simply a request for more information.

Bo Bennett

Every sale has five basic obstacles: no need, no money, no hurry, no desire, no trust.

- Zig Ziglar

Obstacles don't have to stop you. If you run into a wall, don't turn around and give up. Figure out how to climb it, go through it or work around it.

Michael Jackson

Customer normally try to LOCK the Sales Process at this stage

No one wants to be SOLD. Everybody tries to buy a product or service to fulfil some <u>unfulfilled needs.</u> So, when you are presenting your product to the customer – he is simultaneously creating a picture in his mind about – how can this product or service take care of my unfulfilled need/s.

The KEY to unlock the basic objections

The Key to understanding what is going on in mind of the Customer – is simply to ask a few QUESTIONS – in a sequence – which will help you to understand the Customers picture in mind and will allow you to design your STATEMENT / ANSWER which will endorse the reason why he should go for your product

6 Step Objection Handling Technique

1. Understanding the Customers query

2. Re-stating to clarify

3. Making the basic objection as the final objection

4. Asking "WHY"? (SILENT)

5. Answering sequence.... (BY You, after listening to the answer of the Customer "Why")

6. Supporting with a minor decision

Let's see this in the form of a conversation with the customer

BASIC OBJECTIONS raised by customers (and how these 6 steps work)

-   **NO TRUST**

-   **NO HURRY**

-   **NO MONEY**

-   **NO NEED**

-   **NO TRUST**

-   You need to remember 6 steps always

-   Normally your mental temperature rises to +1200 degrees at this point.... because you know he is unwilling to close the deal.

-   Keep yourself cool (minus) -1200 degree at this point

    Address the Client with a SMILE

-   **Objection: <u>NO TRUST</u> (6 Steps Objection handling)**

1. (Nod) – yes, Sir, you have asked a very valid question?

2. If I have correctly understood you – you do not have faith in private finance companies?

3. Is this the only issue bothering you to invest in our plan?

4. **WHY? (Keep SILENT** – Wait for the Clients answer ......do not speak at all at this stage.... if you can build at least 7 seconds of silence.... the Customer will start talking...do not interrupt.... just listen carefully what he is saying...and built your Logical answer sequence)

5. Now give Your Logical answer to his explanation....

6. **"YOU ARE BUYING A PEACE OF MIND FROM US"** – if I could have been in your place I will blindly go for my protection.

- **Objection: NO HURRY**

- Indirectly the Customer is asking: **Why is it so urgent to buy it NOW?**

  - To deal with **NO HURRY** situations

  - You must use **Motivational stories (Someone** delayed – met an accident – died – now the family is in soup**)**

    And

  - **Delay in Purpose (EMERALD purpose)**

- **NO MONEY**

  - **NO MONEY & NO HURRY are the two sides of the same coin**

  - If the client says... "You come after some time" – i.e... showing No Hurry

  - Immediately say – "Is it because of the money?"

  - Normally Client says "Yes"

- Ask "How much can you invest?" – get some commitment amount

- Ask at this stage the Full Annual Premium

- If the client says it's difficult – now show him the half-yearly premium & keep SILENT – wait for 7 seconds – if he agrees to go for the deal.

- If he disagrees – tell him the quarterly premium – keep SILENT for 7 seconds – see his reaction

- NEVER tell all the Annual, Half-yearly, Quarterly premium at once. Go step by step.

- Handling a **NO NEED** situation

Use 3 F – Formula

- **FEEL**

- **FELT**

- **FOUND**

Feel, felt & found are 3 stages in a buyer's life

Say like this "Sir just like you I also **FEEL** at one time that I don't NEED INSURANCE"

"Then when one of my friends took me through the EMERALD List – I understood my liability as a sensible man – I **FELT** that I need to be covered by a Life Insurance Policy"

"Today I have covered my EMERALD List – and I **FOUND** myself at the top of the world having extreme peace of mind – if anything happens in my life – my family will still sustain its own lifestyle and ambitions".

« Chapter 9 »

Negotiation skills

In business, you don't get what you deserve, you get what you negotiate. - Chester L. Karrass

"Let us never negotiate out of fear. But let us never fear to negotiate.
— John F. Kennedy

"Negotiation is not about figuring out who is right or wrong. It is about getting the parties involved to agree to embrace the other party's perspective."
— Elizabeth Suarez

Negotiation is a stage where the buyer and the seller must agree on a WIN WIN Situation.

The various FEATURES and RIDERS of the PLAN which you can "ADD" or "DELETE" to a policy are given to you to negotiate with the customer and bring him to a stage where he agrees with some or all or none.

So, to exercise this negotiation skill you need to ask **Close–ended Question…**where the answer of the customer will end with **"Yes" or "No"**

- **Negotiation begins** – when the Customer says a lot of "YES" in your close-ended questions when you are **validating** the **EMERALD List**

- **Negotiation is to fix the Design of the product** – what the Final policy look like with riders or without riders

- **Negotiation is to fix the Premium** – whether it will be Annual or Half yearly or Quarterly or Monthly

- **Negotiation is to fix the Date and Mode Payment** – whether you will accept Cheque or Demand Draft or Cash – all these points are negotiable

- **Negotiation is a Win–Win situation**

Situation	You Lose	You Win
I Win	**Win-Lose**	**Win-Win**
I Lose	**Lose-Lose**	**Lose-Win**

BATNA – Negotiation Model

BATNA stands for

- **B = Better**

- **A = Alternative**

- **T = To a**

- **N = Negotiated**

- **A = Agreement**

What does it mean and how we can apply this is our sales process

- **Design the High-End Product** – this means add all features and riders and approach the customer and see his comfort level as per EMERALD list

- **Start with a High Premium to negotiate**

- Your **BETTER ALTERNATIVE (BA)** – may be a TERM Policy of the same sum assured where the premium is very low – but you are proposing an endowment policy with a very high premium.

- Let the customer decide to what extent he can pay the premium – the customer's SWEET SPOT – **the NEGOTIATED AGREEMENT (NA) – I WIN YOU WIN**

- **Now, fix the payment date to-day – or take a commitment**

The SKILL required here is to Scale Down to the Comfort Zone of the Customer

- **When you Negotiate with the Design, Premium & Date parameters**

- **Customer says "No" – in most of the step**

- **Allow him to ventilate**

- **Now ask – "What minimum Design you want in the Policy with Riders or without Riders, how much would you like to pay and when?"**

Your Sales presentation is basically a conversation with a customer where according to Albert Mehrabian, a personal communication normally has the following impact on the other person

7% of Words

38% of Tone and energy of your voice

55% of Body Language (Non-verbal)

So, in a personal communication, your 7% Words that you use makes some meaning to the Customer – rest 93% (i.e... 38% Tone + 55% Body

Language) – help the customer to decide whether to buy from you or not.

Our bodies speak louder than our words

Similarly, the Customers body language & his tone also help you to understand when the customer is ready to buy, and he will give you a lot of non-verbal signals to close the deal

Body Language of the customer and his buying Signals

- He puts on his glasses, he begins to study your proposal.

- He asks questions.

- He begins to calculate the benefits.

- He becomes friendlier towards you.

- He co-operates better

- He indicates concern about his EMERALD problem.

- He pulls his chair up closer.

- He leans forward.

- He begins to pay closer attention.

- His tone of voice changes.

- He becomes involved

- He scratches his head, rubs his chin, nods his head.

- His facial expression reveals concern.

- He asks questions as if he had made the purchase.

- He asks about how to pay.

- He asks about the medical examination - i.e. What doctor?

- He asks questions like "Can I pay half-yearly?"

- He asks the question like "Can I stop paying after 10 years?"

Result

- You find – the Customer ends up saying more than Your expectation

- **The Customer comes forward to CLOSE the Deal.** (It is not happening to you now, because you are trying the sell the plan – and not selling the plan to suit his PURPOSE & BUDGET – try to SELL on the PURPOSE)

« Chapter 10 »

CLOSE A DEAL

"Confidence and enthusiasm are the greatest sales producers in any kind of economy." O.B. SMITH

"You don't close a sale; you open a relationship if you want to build a long term, successful enterprise." PATRICIA FRIPP

"Take more chances than you dare. You'll make more sales than you expect. That's the formula." Jeffrey Gitomer

ABC of Closing = Always Be Closing

It means always be ready to close a deal. Sometimes Customer might have done a lot of research and homework beforehand and is only asking for this much Sum Assure for these many years of premium payment term — how much is your premium — these are situations where customer is already in a closing stage — just close the deal by forwarding the proposal form and then tell the premium.

In this chapter, we will discuss, frequently used closing techniques which are low risk in nature and once you master them — it will help you to enjoy and close sales one after the other.

- **LOW-RISK CLOSING Techniques**

The Concept of Balance Sheet Closing

BANK DEPOSIT	INSURANCE PREMIUM
If you put in your bank account	- Keep Rs 10000
- Keep Rs 10,000	- Yearly return 6-10%
- Interest 6% = Rs 600	
	- If somebody dies after one year – his family gets minimum at least 200,000 – 10,000,000 - (depending upon what kind of policy – endowment or term, the age of entry and total policy term
- Total Rs 10600	
- If somebody dies after one year – his family gets Rs 10600	

Now, you understand at every stage of your life to attain the EMERALD Goals – you are always financially more secure than keeping the money in the bank

Ben Franklin Closing technique

XYZ Insurance	ABC Insurance
- Age: 30	- Age: 30
- Term: 20	- Term: 20
- Premium:Rs 4895	- Premium:Rs 4895
- S.A. Rs 401,390	- S.A. Rs 100,000

Here the premium is same – but the Sum Assured Coverage is different. It is the comparison between 2 same Financial Instrument ie. Insurance Products only.

Now attempt the SUMMARY CLOSING TECHNIQUE

<u>**Preference**</u> : "So, Sir You <u>**prefer**</u> …………Plan (Name of the Plan)"

<u>**Choice**</u> : "And your <u>**choice**</u> is to take it for ………number of years ?, right"

<u>**Add-on**</u> : " And you want to <u>**add on**</u> the following Riders …….."

<u>**Trial Offer**</u> : " And your premium amount is coming to ………….."

<u>**Loaded "YES"**</u> : In All the above questions if his answer "Yes" , "Yes" , "Yes" , "Yes" and "Yes"……..**then he is ready to buy now**…..this technique is also known as **5 "Yes" Technique**….at least ask him five definite questions where he agrees with your proposal

This stage is also known as **"Trial Proposal" Stage**

Hand him over the Proposal Form & show him where all the sign……if he is taking the Form from you and search for a pen or take your pen and ready to sign…. You make a DEAL……..this is stage is called **SELF Close Stage.**

Additionally, go to the Health section of the Form and start asking Heath related issues – if he is eagerly answering …he is ready to BUY.

At this stage you can ask him some **"Minor Points"** …when you are likely to go for a Medical Test (if required) or who will be your nominee etc.

Finally, **Ask for the Cheque / Premium / Money**

Summary of Closing techniques

1.   **Balance Sheet Close**
2.   **Ben Franklin Close**
3.   **Preference Close**
4.   **Choice Close**
5.   **Add-on Close**
6.   **Trial Close**
7.   **Loaded "Yes" Close or**
8.   **5 "Yes" Close**

9. Trial Proposal Close - <u>**Hand him over the Proposal Form**</u>
10. Health Close
11. Minor Point Close
12. Ask for the Cheque / Premium / Money

« Chapter 11 »

Policy delivery

"If a child, a spouse, a life partner, or a parent depends on you and your income, you need life insurance." - Suze Orman

A man who dies without adequate life insurance should have to come up and see the mess he created – Will Rogers

Policy delivery is not the sale, it's a breakthrough for a sale, the sale will be completed when the last premium will be paid – Mitash

The biggest mistake every average Insurance Agent does is – after selling the policy to a Customer, they stop contacting them.

We need to SERVICE a SALE

The 4 important objectives in Policy Delivery are as follows:

1. **To resell the need and make the RELATIONSHIP solid**

2. **To condition your client for the next purchase on the EMERALD issues**

3. **To get REFERRED lead information and introductions.**

4. **To enable you to BUILD PROFESSIONAL PRESTIGE for YOURSELF and the COMPANY**

So, once you come to know from your company that the Policy has been delivered – then schedule another appointment with the Client for a Post Delivery explanation of the policy – **The Delivery Interview**

Delivery Interview benefits

- **The delivery interview presents the opportunity to build a solid client relationship with your new policy owner. The method you use, what you say and do and your approach to the delivery interview can affect your persistence, your renewal commissions, and your future sales opportunities.**

- **Establishing A Client forever…. moving towards <u>Customer Loyalty</u>**

- **A policy owner buys only once…A client buys several times… next purchase on the next issue of the EMERALD Needs**

- **Your mission is to <u>build clients forever.</u>**

The delivery interview process includes these points:

- Congratulate the client for taking a decision to cover his/her EMERALD needs

- Explain the Policy benefits from the Policy Bond

- Explain some policy provisions…Always advise a Client to inform about his policy details to his/her Family Members

- Explain premium schedule

- Render a distinct service…. give him/her the assurance, that you will be calling every month at least once to keep in touch…so no worries.

- Discuss next purchase

- Get referred leads to new prospects – at least 2 Referred Leads

- Repeat your congratulations

Now just step back and think for Yourself

- How many of you are having a Life Insurance Policy?

- Have you ever thought of your EMERALD Needs before?

- Have you covered any one of the EMERALD Needs?

- If you have any Policy, after selling the Policy to you – did your agent come back to you to explain the Bond?

- Did your agent at least call on you to check whether you have received the Bond?

- Has he created any bondage & relationship with you?

- Do you want to REPEAT the same MISTAKE that your AGENT did with you?

- Remember – the receipt of the first check is the Breakthrough of a Sale – the sale gets closed after 20 / 30 years when the last premium is paid – Any gap in your Relationship can damage the entire Business – Your loyal Customer can move to a Competitor for better SERVICE by surrendering the Policy.

« Chapter 12 »

Service After Sales

"Coming together is a beginning.
Keeping together is progress.
Working together is success."
- Henry Ford

"Customers don't expect you to be perfect. They do expect you to fix
things when they go wrong."
- Donald Porter V.P., British Airways

"Being on par in terms of price and quality only gets you into the
game. Service wins the game."
- Tony Alessandra

- **BUILDING A PERMANENT CAREER** ON A PROFESSIONAL
  Platform depends on:

- **Quality Business – end to end <u>COMMUNICATION</u> with the CLIENT**
- **Impeccable Service – <u>RESPONDING</u> to every CALL of the CLIENT**

- **Creating Loyal Customer Base – continuous <u>TOUCH</u> with the CLIENT**

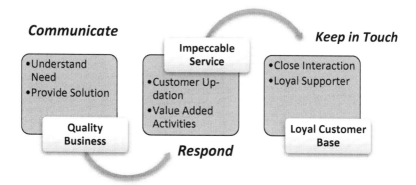

- Another advantage of good servicing lies in repeat sales.

- Most successful financial advisers derive from 25% to 85% of their business from people who have previously bought from them.

- **Quality policy-owners are excellent Centers of influence**

  If you have really understood the **EMERALD NEED** of the Customer & provided genuine SOLUTION – these Quality Policy Owners become very good COI (Centre Of Influence) and will give you qualified leads

---

We need to maintain 3-Phase Service Program

- **Phase I: Maintain a 12 Point Contact With Your Clients**

- **Phase II: Do an Annual Service Call – Business Call – Reminder for premium Payment**

- **Phase III: Provide Continuous Service – updating with latest**

  regulatory changes and economic impacts.

Phase I: Maintain a 12 Point Contact with Your Clients

- Record information about your policy owner that will give you an opportunity to make contact at various times of the year, such as ...

- -Birth-dates of family members

- -Policy anniversary [thanks and congratulations]

- -Wedding Anniversary

- -New Year and other Holidays

- -Promotion, Graduation, and other special occasions

- Send a card, a simple note, or even a small, inexpensive gift. It would be practical to send something:

a. -personal

b. -useful

c. -with your name on it

Maintain this Excel sheet for 12 Point Contact over all the 12 months with the Client on various reasons, so that they always remember you and whenever the client is discussing anything regarding Life Insurance with his/her friends and relatives – he will remember you and you score to get a **HOT LEAD.**

12 Point Contact Call Sheet

Name of Customer	Jan	Feb	Mar	Apr	May	June	July	Aug	Sep	Oct	Nov	Dec
	Various reasons to call & keep in touch with every Client (Customer Engagement Plan)											
1. Mr. X As an Example, Call over 12 months	Birthday Wish Call	Marriage Anniversary Call	Congrats on Promotion Call	Annual Premium Reminder Call (Official Call)	Call to ensure receipt of premium	Call to inform Regulatory Changes	Call to wish his Son's birthday	Call to inform launch of a New Plan	Call to invite in a Customer Meet	Call to wish for some Festival	Call to take some advice on personal issues	Call to take another set of Referrals
2.												
3.												
4.												
5.												
... .	Keep adding for every Customer											

Keep adding more rows to accommodate every Client.

Phase II: Do an Annual Service Call

- An average policy owner buys at least four policies during his lifetime.

- Schedule an annual service calls on your clients to upgrade their insurance coverage.

- Limra Study: A large number of buyers of life insurance indicate a strong willingness to buy again a year or two after the sale.

Opportunities for Resale

- File Update – based on EMERALD Needs

- Changes in Economic or Social Circumstances

a.   –an increase in salary

b.   –promotion

c.   –a new member of the family

Phase III: Provide Continuous Service

- Remember that continuous service minimizes lapses.

- It protects your client's family, your company's reputation, and your personal income

- "GETTING A CLIENT IS IMPORTANT TODAY BUT KEEPING HIM IS EVEN MORE IMPORTANT TO YOUR FUTURE!"

The Concept of Good Servicing is to : <u>SERV – ICE</u>

<u>SERV – ICE means</u>

Serve Customer

- **INFORMATION**
- **COMMUNICATION**
- **ENTERTAINMENT**

Serving INFORMATION:

What are the kinds of Information you think you can provide to the Customer through-out the year?

Through-out 12 months you need to find ways to feed the Customer with New & Helpful Information which will value-add to the Customer's life.

Keep the 12 Point Contact MATRIX for Calling Customer every month

You need to maintain this kind of a Calling Matrix to keep your Customer up-dated. The more you call up your Customer & help them build better Financial Portfolio – the closer you become to the customer – you create a LOYAL CUSTOMER BASE.

COMMUNICATION:

What are the various ways you can Communicate to your Customer?

You can communicate with your customer through various channels.

- Direct Phone Call
- Face to face informal meet (Remember you are meeting informally & the only objective is to provide more INFORMATION to the Customer & NOT SELLING)
- E-mail communication
- Over Social Media Chatting (Facebook etc.)
- By Mail
- Over Skype
- By SMS
- Social gathering
- Party mix-up

ENTERTAINMENT:

How can you Entertain your Customer?

Keeping the Customer base entertained – itself creates a huge excitement. The best strategies to be applied here are:

- Drawing competition for children
- Small informal get together
- Small Picnic
- Sending Movie Tickets

Mitash Bhattacharyya

- Sending tickets for a Music concert
- Getting a pass for a Cricket/ Football Match
- Giving away Holiday Coupons

Remember – this is **YOUR BUSINESS** – YOU NEED to **BUILD Your Own EMPIRE**.

25 minutes to analyse the EMERALD Needs

10 minutes to present your Plan based on EMERALD Needs

5 minutes to close with at least 5 closing techniques – Enjoy ……

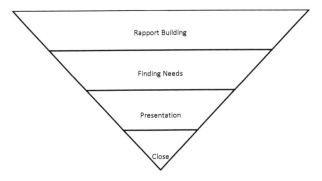

Wish You All the BEST

About Author

Mitash Bhattacharyya is a Learning & Development Professional focussed mainly on enhancing People's Competency to do their Job flawlessly to produce the desire RESULTS.

He is an MBA and ALP (Accelerated Leadership Program) from IIM-Ahmadabad and a Certified E-Learning Professional.

He has over 31 + years of work experience in India, Dubai, Doha, and Muscat & Sri Lanka.

He worked in Fortune 500 Companies like Allianz-Bajaj and Aviva demanding companies like Wipro and was associated with Brands like PENTAX, AESCULAP FUJI, HELLIGE and automobile brands like TOYOTA, LEXUS, FORD, LINCOLN, KIA, MAN, HINO, KOMATSU etc.

He worked in various capacities in different sectors like
- Automobile
- Life Insurance
- Health-Care & Hospital
- Education
- FMCG
- Power Sector &
- Real Estate & Construction Chemicals

Based on Balance Score Card and its Business parameter – he provides Learning Curriculum on Training and Business Development to produce profitable Business Results. The Training methodology he adopts – will bring permanent CHANGE in the participant's Job behaviour and put Learning into their Long-term memory & Re-Call System guaranteeing a Higher Level of PRODUCTIVITY to achieve the Business Objectives – which can be measured, captured and reviewed through Balance Score Card.

Visit : wwwmitash2000.com

Made in the USA
Middletown, DE
21 October 2024

62911522R00049